WILLIAM WORDSWORTH: A CHRONOLOGICAL TABLE OF HIS LIFE

1770	Born 7 April at Cockermouth.
1771	Birth of sister Dorothy on Christmas
1778	Death of mother, Anne Wordsworth,
1779-87	At Hawkshead Grammar School.
1783	Death of father John Wordsworth; Lowther.
1787-91	At St. John's College, Cambridge.
1791-92	In France during Revolution. Affair wi a daughter Anne-Caroline.
1795	With sister Dorothy at Racedown, Dorset. Met Coleridge.
1797	Moved to Alfoxden, Holford in Somerset, to be near Coleridge at Nether Stowey. Compiled *Lyrical Ballads*.
1799	Moved with Dorothy to Dove Cottage, Grasmere.
1802	Married Mary Hutchinson.
1803-10	Birth of five children to Wordsworths: John, Dora, Thomas, Catharine and William.
1805	Brother John drowned in a shipwreck off south coast of England.
1808	Moved to Allan Bank. Estrangement with Coleridge.
1810	Moved to Old Rectory, Grasmere.
1812	Death of Catharine and Thomas.
1813	Appointed Distributor of Stamps for Westmorland. Moved to Rydal Mount.
1834	S. T. Coleridge died.
1841	Dora Married Edward Quillinan
1842	Civil List pension.
1843	Southey died; Wordsworth succeeded him to poet laureateship.
1847	Dora Quillinan died.
1850	On 23 April, Wordsworth died. Buried at Grasmere churchyard.
1855	Dorothy Wordsworth died at Rydal Mount, and buried at Grasmere.
1859	Mary Wordsworth, the poet's wife, died. Buried at Grasmere.

* * *

FURTHER READING

William Wordsworth, a Biography in two volumes, by Mary Moorman: 1) *The Early Years* 1770-1803; 2) *The Later Years* 1803-1850 (first published: vol., I 1957, and vol., II 1965 by the Clarendon Press).

Wordsworth Poetical Works, edited by Thos. Hutchinson; a new edition revised by Ernest de Selincourt (published by Oxford University Press 1969).

Wordsworth and Coleridge—A Study of their Literary Relations in 1801-1802, by William Heath (published by Clarendon Press, 1970).

Recollections of the Lakes and the Lake Poets by Thos. de Quincey, with Introduction by David Wright (published by Penguin Books 1972).

Home at Grasmere, the Grasmere Journal of Dorothy Wordsworth, edited by Colette Clark (published by Penguin Books, 1960).

Wordsworth's Guide to the Lakes, with Introduction etc., by Ernest de Selincourt (fifth edition published by Oxford University Press, 1970).

William Wordsworth 1770-1970. edited by Nesta Clutterbuck (printed for the Trustees of Dove Cottage by Lund Humphries, Bradford and London 1970).

CONTENTS

		Pages
Introduction		
Prophets of Nature	Two Tributes	1
Cockermouth	Wordsworth's Birthplace & River Derwent	2
	'Fair Seed-time had my soul. . . .'	3
	'The Sparrow's Nest'	3
	'The Spirit of Cockermouth Castle'	4
Hawkshead	Hawkshead Grammar School	4
	Hawkshead Revisited	5
Vale of Esthwaite	Early Morning	6
Windermere	Rowing on the Lake	6
Furness Fells	'Nuns Fret not at their Convents. . . .'	7
Grasmere	'On Nature's Invitation Do I Come. . . .'	7
	'Thou See'st a Homely Pile. . . .'	8
	Personal Talk	9
	'To Joanna'	10
	'Point Rash-Judgement'	12
	'Fir Grove'	14
	Grisedale Tarn	15
	'A Farewell'	15
Helvellyn	A First Ascent	16
Ullswater	'I Wandered Lonely as a Cloud. . . .'	18
	'Airey-Force'	18
Applethwaite	'Beaumont! It Was Thy Wish. . . .'	19
Wansfell	'Wansfell! This Household Has a Favoured Lot. . . .'	20
Ambleside	'While Beams of Orient Light. . . .'	21
Rydal	'By the Side of Rydal Mere'	21
	The Far Terrace	22
	'Adieu! Rydalian Laurels. . . .'	22
Kirkstone Pass	'The Pass of Kirkstone'	23
Brothers Water	'The Cock is Crowing. . . .'	25
River Eden	'The River Eden, Cumberland'	26
Lowther	'Lowther! in Thy Majestic Pile. . . .'	27
Duddon River	'Child of the Clouds! . . .'	28
	'Kirk of Ulpha'	28
	'Afterthought'	28
Epilogue	'An Evening Walk'	29

ILLUSTRATIONS

Grasmere Lake, by John Laporte, 1795	Cover
William Wordsworth, by B. R. Haydon, 1818	Frontispiece

Wordsworth House, Cockermouth
The Ferry on Windermere Lake, by John Smith, 1792
Dove Cottage in Wordsworth's Time, by Dora Wordsworth
View of Grasmere, by T. Austin, 1839
Keswick Lake, Cumberland, by J. M. W. Turner R.A., 1837
Ambleside, Westmorland, by Thos. C. Dibdin, 1852
Rydal Mount, by T. L. Aspland, 1849
Ullswater, Cumberland, by J. M. W. Turner R.A., 1835

—::—

ACKNOWLEDGEMENTS

Illustrations are reproduced by kind permission of

Mr. Kenneth Smith, ex-librarian, Carlisle; now of Adel, Leeds—
Grasmere Lake, by John Laporte, 1795
The Ferry on Windermere, by John Smith, 1792
Ullswater, Cumberland, by J. M. W. Turner, 1835
Keswick Lake, by J. M. W. Turner, 1837
The National Portrait Gallery, London—
William Wordsworth, by B. R. Haydon, 1818
The National Trust, North-west Region—
Wordsworth House, Cockermouth
View of Grasmere, by T. Austin, 1839
The Trustees of Dove Cottage, Grasmere—
Dove Cottage in Wordsworth's Time, by Dora Wordsworth
The Armitt Trust, Ambleside—
Rydal Mount, by T. L. Aspland, 1849

—◆—

©**Richard J. Hutchings 1996**
(1922 - 1991)

ISBN 0 9504736 1 8

First Edition 1977
Tenth Impression 2006

Published by Rydall Mount and Gardens
Ambleside, Cumbria, LA22 9LU – Tel: 015394 33002

Printed by Biltmore Printers, 14 Manners View, Newport, Isle of Wight, PO30 5FA

Dedicated to my dear friends
The Misses Elliott
Of Appleby-in-Westmorland

INTRODUCTION

William Wordsworth's poetry and life in the Lake District have contributed perhaps as much as anything else to Cumbria's universal appeal. His memory haunts every track, every fell and lake, all of which he knew intimately.

This small anthology of his Lakeland poetry is a guide to memorable milestones in the poet's life, and attempts to capture Cumbria's mountain magic. I have chosen mainly descriptive poems about places in Cumbria. They are not necessarily shown in chronological order of publication. But they enable enthusiasts to enjoy Lakeland scenery as he saw it. Also included are relevant passages from the Grasmere Journal of his sister Dorothy, illustrating his dependence on her, in some of his poetry, for recorded details of Nature observed during their walks. Equally invaluable to the poet was the friendship of Samuel Taylor Coleridge, who, until their estrangement, encouraged Wordsworth to produce some of his finest work. Together they were largely responsible for the revival of the Romantic movement in English poetry, seeing themselves as 'Prophets of Nature'.

—R.J.H.

PROPHETS OF NATURE

Two Tributes

To Coleridge (the poet's closest friend)

Prophets of Nature, we to them will speak
A lasting inspiration, sanctified
By reason, blest by faith: what we have loved,
Others will love, and we will teach them how;
Instruct them how the mind of man becomes
A thousand times more beautiful than the earth
On which he dwells, above this frame of things
(Which, 'mid all revolution in the hopes
And fears of men, doth still remain unchanged)
In beauty exiled, as it is itself
Of quality and fabric more divine.

– from *The Prelude*

To Dorothy Wordsworth (the poet's sister)

She, in the midst of all, preserved me still
A Poet, made me seek beneath that name,
And that alone, my office upon earth;
And, lastly, as hereafter will be shown,
If willing audience fail not, Nature's self,
By all varieties of human love
Assisted, led me back through opening day
To those sweet counsels between head and heart
Whence grew that genuine knowledge, fraught with peace,
Which through the later sinkings of this cause,*
Hath still upheld me, and upholds me now
In the catastrophe....

– from *The Prelude*

*The French Revolution

COCKERMOUTH

Wordsworth's Birthplace by the River Derwent

Wordsworth House is a remarkably well-preserved Georgian dwelling at Cockermouth in the north-west of Cumbria. The terrace at the bottom of the garden overlooks the River Derwent. In this house the poet was born, and the delightful surroundings left an indelible impression on his mind which he recalled with great pleasure in later years.

Was it for this
That one, the fairest of all rivers, loved
To blend his murmurs with my nurse's song,
And, from his alder shades and rocky falls,
And from his fords and shallows, sent a voice
That flowed along my dreams? For this, didst thou,
O Derwent! winding among grassy holms
Where I was looking on, a babe in arms,
Make ceaseless music that composed my thoughts
To more than infant softness, giving me
Amid the fretful dwellings of mankind
A foretaste, a dim earnest, of the calm
That Nature breathes among the hills and groves.

When he had left the mountains and received
On his smooth breast the shadow of those towers
That yet survive, a shattered monument
Of feudal sway, the bright blue river passed
Along the margin of our terrace walk;
A tempting playmate whom we dearly loved.
Oh, many a time have I, a five years' child,
In a small mill-race severed from his stream
Made one long bathing of a summer's day;
Basked in the sun, and plunged and basked again
Alternate, all a summer's day, or scoured
The sandy fields, leaping through flowery groves
Of yellow ragwort; or when rock and hill,
The woods, and distant Skiddaw's lofty height,
Were bronzed with deepest radiance, stood alone
Beneath the sky, as if I had been born
On Indian plains, and from my mother's hut
Had run abroad in wantonness, to sport,
A naked savage, in the thunder shower.

COCKERMOUTH

    Fair seed-time had my soul, and I grew up
Fostered alike by beauty and by fear:
Much favoured in my birth place, and no less
In that beloved Vale to which ere long
We were transplanted—there we were let loose
For sports of wider range. Ere I had told
Ten birthdays, when among the mountain-slopes
Frost, and the breath of frosty wind, had snapped
The last autumnal crocus, 'twas my joy
With store of springes o'er my shoulder hung
To range the open heights where woodcocks run
Among the smooth green turf. . . .

                                  – from *The Prelude*

            *   *   *

'The Sparrow's Nest'

Behold, within the leafy shade,
Those bright blue eggs together laid!
On me the chance-discovered sight
Gleamed like a vision of delight.
I started—seeming to espy
The home and sheltered bed,
The Sparrow's dwelling, which, hard by
My Father's house, in wet or dry
My sister Emmeline* and I
    Together visited.

She looked at it and seemed to fear it;
Dreading, tho' wishing, to be near it:
Such heart was in her, being then
A little Prattler among men.
The Blessing of my later years
Was with me when a boy:
She gave me eyes, she gave me ears;
And humble cares, and delicate fears;
A heart, the fountain of sweet tears;
    And love, and thought, and joy.

*Wordsworth's sister, Dorothy.

COCKERMOUTH

'Address from the Spirit of Cockermouth Castle'

'Thou look'st upon me, and dost fondly think,
Poet! that, stricken as both are by years,
We, differing once so much, are now Compeers,
Prepared, when each has stood his time, to sink
Into the dust. Erewhile a sterner link
United us; when thou, in boyish play,
Entering my dungeon, didst become a prey
To soul-appalling darkness. Not a blink
Of light was there;—and thus did I, thy Tutor,
Make thy young thoughts acquainted with the grave;
While thou wert chasing the winged butterfly
Through my green courts; or climbing, a bold suitor,
Up to the flowers whose golden progeny
Still round my shattered brow in beauty wave.'

* * *

HAWKSHEAD

In 1776/7 William Wordsworth attended Anne Birkett's infant school at Penrith, but after his mother's death he lodged with Ann Tyson at Hawkshead where he attended the Grammar School founded by Edwin Sandys in 1585. The Headmaster, a particularly able teacher, was the Reverend William Taylor. He soon recognized Wordsworth's talents for poetic composition, and a great friendship and understanding developed between them. But the poet's father died in 1783, leaving the five children under the guardianship of Richard Wordsworth and Christopher Crackanthorp. Nevertheless the years at Hawkshead were some of the happiest in William's life.

The Hawkshead Grammar School

... Noble Sandys, inspir'd with great design,
Reared Hawkshead's happy roof, and call'd it mine.
There have I loved to show the tender age
The golden precepts of the classic page;

HAWKSHEAD

To lead the mind to those Elysian plains
Where, throned in gold, immortal Science reigns;
Fair to the view is sacred Truth display'd,
In all the majesty of light array'd,
To teach, on rapid wings, the curious soul
To roam from heaven to heaven, from pole to pole,
From thence to search the mystic cause of things
And follow Nature to her secret springs. . . .

– from *'Lines Written as a School Exercise
at Hawkshead, aged 14 years'*

After leaving the Grammar School Wordsworth took his BA at St John's College, Cambridge. However, he never forgot his Lakeland friends whom he visited on one vacation from the university.

Hawkshead Revisited
(Returning by way of the Windermere ferry)

Bright was the summer's noon when quickening steps
Followed each other till a dreary moor
Was crossed, a bare ridge clomb, upon whose top
Standing alone, as from a rampart's edge,
I overlooked the bed of Windermere,
Like a vast river, stretching in the sun.
With exultation, at my feet I saw
Lake, islands, promontories, gleaming bays,
A universe of Nature's fairest forms
Proudly revealed with instantaneous burst,
Magnificent, and beautiful, and gay.
I bounded down the hill shouting amain
For the old Ferryman; to the shout the rocks
Replied, and when the Charon of the flood
Had staid his oars, and touched the jutting pier,
I did not step into the well-known boat
Without a cordial greeting. Thence with speed
Up the familiar hill I took my way
Towards the sweet Valley*, where I had been reared;
'Twas but a short hour's walk, ere veering round
I saw the snow-white church upon her hill
Sit like a thron'd Lady, sending out
A gracious look all over her domain.

*Hawkshead

HAWKSHEAD

Yon azure smoke betrays the lurking town;
With eager footsteps I advance and reach
The cottage threshold where my journey closed.
Glad welcome had I, with some tears, perhaps,
From my old Dame*, so kind and motherly,
While she perused me with a parent's pride.
The thoughts of gratitude shall fall like dew
Upon thy grave, good creature! While my heart
Can beat never will I forget thy name....
– from *The Prelude*

*Ann Tyson of Colthouse near Hawkshead.

* * *

VALE OF ESTHWAITE

Early Morning
Magnificent
The morning rose, in memorable pomp,
Glorious as e'er I had beheld—in front,
The sea lay laughing at a distance; near
The solid mountains shone, bright as the clouds,
Grain-tinctured, drenched in empyrean light;
And in the meadows and lower grounds
Was all the sweetness of a common dawn—
Dews, vapours, and the melody of birds,
And labourers going forth to till the fields....
– from *The Prelude*

LAKE WINDERMERE

Rowing on Windermere
When summer came
Our pastime was, on bright half-holidays,
To sweep along the plain of Windermere
With rival oars; and the selected bourne
Was now an Island musical with birds
That sang and ceased not; now a Sister Isle
Beneath the oaks' umbrageous covert, sown
With lilies of the valley like a field;
And now a third small Island, where survived
In solitude the ruins of a shrine
Once to Our Lady dedicate, and served
Daily with chaunted rites. In such a race
So ended, disappointment could be none,
Uneasiness, or pain, or jealousy:
We rested in the shade, all pleased alike,
Conquered and conqueror.
– from *The Prelude*

FURNESS FELLS

Between the River Duddon and the southern shores of Windermere, below Lake Coniston, are the Furness Fells, the southernmost limits of the Lakelands.

> Nuns fret not at their convent's narrow room;
> And hermits are contented with their cells;
> And students with their pensive citadels;
> Maids at the wheel, the weaver at his loom,
> Sit blithe and happy; bees that soar for bloom,
> High as the highest Peak of Furness-fells,
> Will murmur by the hour in foxglove bells:
> In truth the prison, unto which we doom
> Ourselves, no prison is: and hence for me,
> In sundry moods, 'twas pastime to be bound
> Within the Sonnet's scanty plot of ground;
> Pleased if some Souls (for such there needs must be)
> Who have felt the weight of too much liberty,
> Should find brief solace there, as I have found.
>
> – from *Miscellaneous Sonnets*

VALE OF GRASMERE

Ever since his youth, Wordsworth hoped that one day he would be able to make Grasmere his home. Its beauty was everything a recluse poet desired, and when at last in 1799 Dove Cottage became vacant, his dream was realised. Dove Cottage was formerly an inn by the name of the Dove and Olive Bough.

'*On Nature's Invitation Do I Come. . . .*'

> On Nature's invitation do I come,
> By Reason sanctioned. Can the choice mislead,
> That made the calmest, fairest spot on earth,
> With all its unappropriated good,

My own; and not mine only, for with me
Entrenched—say rather peacefully embowered—
Under yon orchard, in yon humble cot,
A younger orphan of a Home extinct,
The only daughter of my parents dwells:
Aye, think on that, my heart, and cease to stir;
Pause upon that, and let the breathing frame
No longer breathe, but all be satisfied.
Oh, if such silence be not thanks to God
For what hath been bestowed, then where, where then
Shall gratitude find rest? Mine eyes did ne'er
Fix on a lovely object, nor my mind
Take pleasure in the midst of happy thoughts,
But either she, whom now I have, who now
Divides with me this loved abode, was there
Or not far off. Where'er my footsteps turned,
Her voice was like a hidden Bird that sang;
The thought of her was like a flash of light
Or an unseen companionship, a breath
Or fragrance independent of the wind.
In all my goings, in the new and old
Of all my meditations, and in this
Favourite of all, in this the most of all. . . .
Embrace me then, ye hills, and close me in.
Now in the clear and open day I feel
Your guardianship: I take it to my heart;
'Tis like the solemn shelter of the night.
But I would call thee beautiful; for mild,
And soft, and gay, and beautiful thou art,
Dear valley, having in thy face a smile,
Though peaceful, full of gladness. Thou art pleased,
Pleased with thy crags, and woody steeps, thy Lake,
Its one green Island, and its winding shores,
The multitude of little rocky hills,
Thy Church, and cottages of mountain-stone
Clustered like stars some few, but single most,
And lurking dimly in their shy retreats,
Or glancing at each other cheerful looks,
Like separate stars with clouds between.

Grasmere's lake has an island with a stone hut providing shelter for cattle and sheep. In it Wordsworth often found the solitude necessary for undisturbed thought and composition.

Thou see'st a homely Pile, yet to these walls
The heifer comes in the snow-storm, and here
The new-dropped lamb finds shelter from the wind.
And hither does one Poet sometimes row
His pinnace, a small vagrant barge, up-piled

> With plenteous store of heath and withered fern,
> (A lading which he with his sickle cuts
> Among the mountains) and beneath this roof
> He makes his summer couch, and here at noon
> Spreads out his limbs, while, yet unshorn, the Sheep,
> Panting beneath the burthen of their wool
> Lie round him, even as if they were a part
> Of his own Household: nor, while from his bed
> He looks, through the open door-place, toward the lake
> And to the stirring breezes, does he want
> Creations lovely as the work of sleep—
> Fair sights, and visions of romantic joy!
>
> – from *Written on the Isle of Grasmere*

But sometimes he preferred to sit idly beside the kitchen-parlour fire, listening in silence to the flap of the flames,

> I am not One who much or oft delight
> To season my fireside with personal talk,—
> Of friends, who live within an easy walk,
> Or neighbours, daily, weekly, in my sight:
> And, for my chance acquaintance, ladies bright,
> Sons, mothers, maidens withering on the stalk,
> These all wear out of me, like Forms with chalk
> Painted on rich men's floors, for one feast night.
> Better than such discourse doth silence long,
> Long, barren silence, square with my desire;
> To sit without emotion, hope, or aim,
> In the loved presence of my cottage-fire,
> And listen to the flapping of the flame,
> Or kettle whispering its faint undersong. ...
>
> –from *'Personal Talk'*

Contrary to the impression given in the above lines, William Wordsworth was an energetic walker, often doing between 20 and 30 miles in a day. So the whole of the Vale of Grasmere was familiar ground to him, and he liked nothing better than to be accompanied by close friends and relatives. The poem below is addressed to Joanna Hutchinson who had not visited Grasmere since the move into Dove Cottage.

VALE OF GRASMERE

'To Joanna' (the poet's sister-in-law)
Amid the smoke of cities did you pass
The time of early youth; and there you learned,
From years of quiet industry, to love
The living Beings by your own fireside,
With such a strong devotion, that your heart
Is slow to meet the sympathies of them
Who look upon the hills with tenderness,
And make dear friendships with the streams and groves.
Yet we, who are transgressors in this kind,
Dwelling retired in our simplicity
Among the woods and fields, we love you well,
Joanna! and I guess, since you have been,
So distant from us now for two long years,
That you will gladly listen to discourse,
However trivial, if you thence be taught
That they, with whom you once were happy, talk
Familiarly of you and of old times.

While I was seated, now some ten days past,
Beneath those lofty firs that overtop
Their ancient neighbour, the old steeple-tower,
The Vicar from his gloomy house hard by
Came forth to greet me; and, when he had asked,
'How fares Joanna, that wild-hearted Maid!
And when will she return to us?' he paused;
And, after short exchange of village news
He with grave looks demanded for what cause,
Reviving obsolete idolatry,
I, like a Runic Priest, in characters
Of formidable size had chiselled out
Some uncouth name upon the native rock,
Above the Rotha, by the forest-side,
—Now, by those dear immunities of heart
Engendered between malice and true love,
I was not loth to be so catechised,
And this was my reply:—'As it befell,
One summer morning we had walked abroad
At break of day, Joanna and myself.
—'Twas that delightful season when the broom
Full-flowered, and visible on every steep,
Along the copses runs in veins of gold.
Our pathway led us on to Rotha's banks;
And, when we came in front of that tall rock
That eastward looks, I there stopped short—and stood
Tracing the lofty barrier with my eye
From base to summit; such delight I found
To note in shrub and tree, in stone and flower,
That intermixture of delicious hues,

VALE OF GRASMERE

Along so vast a surface, all at once,
In one impression, by connecting force
Of their own beauty, imaged in the heart.
—When I had gazed perhaps two minutes' space,
Joanna, looking in my eyes, beheld
That ravishment of mine, and laughed aloud.
The Rock, like something starting from a sleep,
Took up the Lady's voice, and laughed again;
That ancient Woman seated on Helm-crag
Was ready with her cavern; Hammar-scar,
And the tall Steep of Silver-how, sent forth
A noise of laughter; southern Loughrigg heard,
And Fairfield answered with a mountain tone;
Helvellyn far into the clear blue sky
Carried the Lady's voice,—old Skiddaw blew
His speaking-trumpet;—back out of the clouds
Of Glaramara southward came the voice;
And Kirkstone tossed it from his misty head.
—Now whether (said I to our cordial Friend,
Who in the heyday of astonishment
Smiled in my face) this were in simple truth
A work accomplished by the brotherhood
Of ancient mountains, or my ear was touched
With dreams and visionary impulses
To me alone imparted, sure I am
That there was a loud uproar in the hills,
And, while we both were listening, to my side
The fair Joanna drew, as if she wished
To shelter from some object of her fear.
—And hence, long afterwards, when eighteen moons
Were wasted, as I chanced to walk alone
Beneath this rock, at sunrise, on a calm
And silent morning, I sat down, and there,
In memory of affections old and true,
I chiselled out in those rude characters
Joanna's name deep in the living stone:—
And I, and all who dwell by my fireside,
Have called the lovely rock, Joanna's Rock.'

VALE OF GRASMERE

In the poem 'Point Rash-judgement' Wordsworth describes the walk round the eastern shore of Lake Grasmere as it was in 1800, now the main road to Ambleside. The two beloved friends mentioned in the poem were, of course, his sister, Dorothy, and his intimate friend, Coleridge, who stayed with them at Dove Cottage over long periods.

'Point Rash-Judgement'

A narrow girdle of rough stones and crags,
A rude and natural causeway, interposed
Between the water and a winding slope.
Of copse and thicket, leaves the eastern shore
Of Grasmere safe in its own privacy:
And there myself and two beloved Friends,
One calm September morning, ere the mist
Had altogether yielded to the sun,
Sauntered on this retired and difficult way.
—Ill suits the road with one in haste; but we
Played with our time; and as we strolled along,
It was our occupation to observe
Such objects as the waves had tossed ashore—
Feather, or leaf, or weed, or withered bough,
Each on the other heaped, along the line
Of the dry wreck. And, in our vacant mood,
Not seldom did we stop to watch some tuft
Of dandelion seed or thistle's beard,
That skimmed the surface of the dead calm lake,
Suddenly halting now—a lifeless stand!
And starting off again with freak as sudden;
In all its sportive wanderings, all the while,
Making report of an invisible breeze
That was its wings, its chariot, and its horse,
Its playmate, rather say, its moving soul.
—And often, trifling with a privilege
Alike indulged to all, we paused, one now,
And now the other, to point out, perchance
To pluck, some flower or water-weed, too fair
Either to be divided from the place
On which it grew, or to be left alone
To its own beauty. Many such there are,
Fair ferns and flowers, and chiefly that tall fern,
So stately, of the Queen Osmunda named;
Plant lovelier, in its own retired abode
On Grasmere's beach, than Naiad by the side
Of Grecian brook, or Lady of the Mere.
Sole-sitting by the shores of old romance.
—So fared we that bright morning: from the fields
Meanwhile, a noise was heard, the busy mirth
Of reapers, men and women, boys and girls.
Delighted much to listen to those sounds,

VALE OF GRASMERE

And feeding thus our fancies, we advanced
Along the indented shore; when suddenly,
Through a thin veil of glittering haze was seen
Before us, on a point of jutting land,
The tall and upright figure of a Man
Attired in peasant's garb, who stood alone,
Angling beside the margin of the lake.
'Improvident and reckless,' we exclaimed,
'The Man must be, who thus can lose a day
Of the mid-harvest, when the labourer's hire
Is ample, and some little might be stored,
Wherewith to cheer him in the winter time.'
Thus talking of that Peasant, we approached
Close to the spot where with his rod and line
He stood alone; whereat he turned his head
To greet us—and we saw a Man worn down
By sickness, gaunt and lean, with sunken cheeks
And wasted limbs, his legs so long and lean
That for my single self I looked at them,
Forgetful of the body they sustained.—
Too weak to labour in the harvest field,
The Man was using his best skill to gain
A pittance from the dead unfeeling lake
That knew not of his wants. I will not say
What thoughts immediately were ours, nor how
The happy idleness of that sweet morn,
With all its lovely images, was changed
To serious musing and to self-reproach.
Nor did we fail to see within ourselves
What need there is to be reserved in speech,
And temper all our thoughts with charity.
—Therefore, unwilling to forget that day,
My Friend, Myself and She who then received
The same admonishment, have called the place
By a memorial name, uncouth indeed.
As e'er by mariner was given to a bay
Or foreland, on a new-discovered coast;
And Point Rash-Judgement is the Name it bears.

The poet's brother, John, was never quite so close to him as Dorothy, until the time he joined them at Dove Cottage. William soon recognized in him his own poetic sensibilities and sensitivity to Nature. But the difference between them was that one could express those feelings, while the other could not. John was a merchant navy captain, trading on the East Indiaman, *Earl of Abergavenny*, but he loved Cumbria as much as his brother and sister and when possible spent home-leave with them.

VALE OF GRASMERE

'Fir-Grove' (an extract)

When thou hadst quitted Esthwaite's pleasant shore,
And taken thy first leave of those green hills
And rocks that were the play-ground of thy youth,
Year followed year, my Brother! and we two,
Conversing not, knew little in what mould
Each other's mind was fashioned; and at length
When once again we met in Grasmere Vale,
Between us there was little other bond
Than common feelings of fraternal love.
But thou, a Schoolboy, to the sea hadst carried
Undying recollections; Nature there
Was with thee; she, who loved us both, she still
Was with thee; and even so didst thou become
A *silent* poet; from the solitude
Of the vast sea didst bring a watchful heart
Still couchant, an inevitable ear,
And an eye practised like a blind man's touch.
—Back to the joyless Ocean thou art gone;
Nor from this vestige of thy musing hours
Could I withhold thy honoured name,—and now
I love the fir-grove with a perfect love.
Thither do I withdraw when cloudless suns
Shine hot, or wind blows troublesome and strong;
And there I sit at evening, when the steep
Of Silver-how, and Grasmere's peaceful lake,
And one green island, gleam between the stems
Of the dark firs, a visionary scene!
And while I gaze upon the spectacle
Of clouded splendour, on this dreamlike sight
Of solemn loveliness, I think on thee,
My Brother, and on all which thou hast lost,
Nor seldom, if I rightly guess, while Thou,
Muttering the verses which I muttered first
Among the mountains, through the midnight watch
Art pacing thoughtfully the vessel's deck
In some far region, here, while o'er my head,
At every impulse of the moving breeze,
The fir-grove murmurs with a sea-like sound.
Alone I tread this path;—for aught I know,
Timing my steps to thine; and, with a store
Of undistinguishable sympathies,
Mingling most earnest wishes for the day
When we, and others whom we love, shall meet
A second time, in Grasmere's happy Vale.

In 1805, however, when John Wordsworth was setting out on his third voyage to the Far East, his vessel was suddenly overwhelmed by a storm

Wordsworth House, Cockermouth

The Ferry on Windermere Lake, by John Smith, 1792

Dove Cottage in Wordsworth's Time, by Dora Wordsworth

View of Grasmere, by T. Austin, 1839

Ullswater, Cumberland, by J. M. W. Turner R.A., 1835

Ambleside, Westmorland, by Thos. C. Dibdin, 1852

Rydal Mount, by T. L. Aspland, 1849

and was wrecked in Weymouth Bay. He went down with his ship, but his body was later retrieved and buried at Wyke in Dorset. William and Dorothy were shattered by the news of his death, and were inconsolable in their grief. The spot where they parted from him was Grisedale Tarn.

Grisedale Tarn

Brother and friend, if verse of mine
Have power to make thy virtues known,
Here let a monumental Stone
Stand—sacred as a Shrine;
And to the few who pass this way,
Traveller or Shepherd, let it say,
Long as these mighty rocks endure,—
Oh do not Thou too fondly brood,
Although deserving of all good,
On any earthly hope, however pure!

– from *Elegiac Verses – In Memory of
my Brother, John Wordsworth*

* * *

A Farewell to Dove Cottage
and Grasmere

Farewell, thou little Nook of mountain-ground,
Thou rocky corner in the lowest stair
Of that magnificent temple which doth bound
One side of our whole vale with grandeur rare;
Sweet garden-orchard, eminently fair,
The loveliest spot that man hath ever found,
Farewell!—we leave thee to Heaven's peaceful care,
Thee, and the Cottage which thou dost surround.

Our boat is safely anchored by the shore,
And there will safely ride when we are gone;
The flowering shrubs that deck our humble door
Will prosper, though untended and alone:

VALE OF GRASMERE

Fields, goods, and far-off chattels we have none:
These narrow bounds contain our private store
Of things earth makes, and sun doth shine upon;
Here are they in our sight—we have no more. . . .

– from '*A Farewell*'

* * *

HELVELLYN

'*To——————— On Her First Ascent to the Summit of Helvellyn*'

Inmate of a mountain-dwelling,
Thou hast clomb aloft, and gazed
From the watch-towers of Helvellyn;
Awed, delighted, and amazed!

Potent was the spell that bound thee
Not unwilling to obey;
For blue Ether's arms, flung round thee,
Stilled the pantings of dismay.

Lo! the dwindling woods and meadows;
What a vast abyss is there!
Lo! the clouds, the solemn shadows,
And the glistenings—heavenly fair!

And a record of commotion
Which a thousand ridges yield;
Ridge, and gulf, and distant ocean
Gleaming like a silver shield!

Maiden! now take flight;—inherit
Alps and Andes—they are thine!
With the morning's roseate Spirit
Sweep their length of snowy line;

Or survey their bright dominions
In the gorgeous colours drest
Flung from off the purple pinions,
Evening spreads throughout the west!

HELVELLYN

Thine are all the choral fountains
Warbling in each sparry vault
Of the untrodden lunar mountains;
Listen to their songs!—or halt,

To Niphates'* top invited,
Whither spiteful Satan steered;
Or descend where the ark alighted,
When the green earth re-appeared;

For the power of hills is on thee,
As was witnessed through thine eye
Then, when old Helvellyn won thee,
To confess their majesty!

*A range of Armenian mountains. In Milton's *Paradise Lost*, Satan set foot there when first he visited the earth.

*   *   *

ULLSWATER

'I Wandered Lonely as a Cloud' is so well-known that it hardly needs introduction. But this may best be accomplished by quoting from Dorothy Wordsworth's Journal for the date Thursday 15 April 1802 describing a walk along the west bank of Ullswater: 'When we were in the woods beyond Gowbarrow park we saw a few daffodils close to the waterside. We fancied that the lake had floated the seeds ashore and that the little colony had so sprung up. But as we went along there were more and yet more and at last under the boughs of the trees, we saw that there was a long belt of them along the shore, about the breadth of a turnpike road. I never saw daffodils so beautiful they grew among the mossy stones about and about them, some rested their heads upon these stones as on a pillow for weariness and the rest tossed and reeled and danced and seemed as if they verily laughed with the wind that blew them over the lake, they looked so gay ever glancing ever changing. This wind blew directly over the lake to them. There was here and there a little knot and a few stragglers

ULLSWATER

a few yards higher up but they were so few as not to disturb the simplicity and unity and life of that one busy highway,' William wrote his poem two years later, no doubt suggested by this record of the event:

'I Wandered Lonely as a Cloud'

I wandered lonely as a cloud
That floats on high o'er vales and hills,
When all at once I saw a crowd,
A host, of golden daffodils;
Beside the lake, beneath the trees,
Fluttering and dancing in the breeze.

Continuous as the stars that shine
And twinkle on the milky way,
They stretched in never-ending line
Along the margin of a bay:
Ten thousand saw I at a glance,
Tossing their heads in sprightly dance.

The waves beside them danced; but they
Out-did the sparkling waves in glee:
A poet could not but be gay,
In such a jocund company:
I gazed—and gazed—but little thought
What wealth the show to me had brought:

For oft, when on my couch I lie
In vacant or in pensive mood,
They flash upon that inward eye
Which is the bliss of solitude;
And then my heart with pleasure fills,
And dances with the daffodils.

'Airey-Force Valley'

——————————— Not a breath of air
Ruffles the bosom of this leafy glen.
From the brook's margin, wide around, the trees
Are steadfast as the rocks; the brook itself,
Old as the hills that feed it from afar,
Doth rather deepen than disturb the calm
Where all things else are still and motionless.
And yet, even now, a little breeze, perchance
Escaped from boisterous winds that rage without,

ULLSWATER

Has entered, by the sturdy oaks unfelt,
But to its gentle touch how sensitive
Is the light ash! that, pendent from the brow
Of yon dim cave, in seeming silence makes
A soft eye-music of slow-waving boughs,
Powerful almost as vocal harmony
To stay the wanderer's steps and soothe his thoughts.

* * *

APPLETHWAITE

Applethwaite is near Keswick at the foot of Skiddaw, one of the most beautiful villages in the Lake District. In 1802 Sir George Beaumont, Wordsworth's admirer, friend and patron presented him with a delightful property in the glen there. Known as the Ghyll, the existing cottage was built in 1867 as indicated by an inscription on its wall. Above and below this date are the two letters WW. This property, now in private hands, is in a setting of a sunlit woodland dell, filled with flowers and green lawns and the sound of cascading waters. Opposite the front of the cottage, a beck tumbles down from its icy source on the slopes of gloomy Skiddaw to a tiny waterfall in view of the windows. The property was given to him so that he could be near his intimate friend Coleridge, who lived with his wife and family at Keswick. But knowing full-well what Coleridge's wife, Sara, thought of the Wordsworths, the poet never built on it himself. He did however write this sonnet to express his gratitude for the present:

'*At Applethwaite, near Keswick*'

Beaumont! it was thy wish that I should rear
A seemly Cottage in this sunny Dell,
On favoured ground, thy gift, where I might dwell
In neighbourhood with One* to me most dear,

*Coleridge

APPLETHWAITE

That undivided we from year to year
Might work in our high calling—a bright hope
To which our fancies, mingling, gave free scope
Till checked by some necessities severe.
And should there slacken, honoured Beaumont! still
Even then we may perhaps in vain implore
Leave of our fate thy wishes to fulfil.
Whether this boon be granted us or not,
Old Skiddaw will look down upon the Spot
With pride, the Muses love it evermore.

WANSFELL

Wansfell is visible from Rydal Mount, a hill to the south-east above Ambleside.

Wansfell! this Household has a favoured lot
Living with liberty on thee to gaze,
To watch while Morn first crowns thee with her rays,
Or when along thy breast serenely float
Evening's angelic clouds. Yet ne'er a note
Hath sounded (shame upon the Bard!) thy praise
For all that thou, as if from heaven, hast brought
Of glory lavished on our quiet days.
Bountiful Son of Earth! when we are gone
From every object dear to mortal sight,
As soon we shall be, may these words attest
How oft, to elevate our spirits, shone
Thy visionary majesties of light,
How in thy pensive glooms our hearts found rest.

AMBLESIDE

When living at Rydal Mount, William Wordsworth was appointed Distributor of Stamps for Westmorland, his office being at Ambleside. The Civil Service appointment began in the year 1813, when he and his family moved from Grasmere to Rydal, and lasted until he acquired a Civil List pension in 1842. In the following year he became Poet Laureate on the death of Robert Southey, his friend at Keswick.

AMBLESIDE

While beams of orient light shoot wide and high,
Deep in the vale a little rural Town
Breathes forth a cloud-like creature of its own,
That mounts not toward the radiant morning sky,
But, with a less ambitious sympathy,
Hangs o'er its Parent waking to the cares,
Troubles and toils that every day prepares.
So Fancy, to the musing Poet's eye,
Endears that Lingerer. And how blest her sway
(Like influence never may my soul reject),
If the calm Heaven, now to its zenith decked
With glorious forms in numberless array,
To the lone shepherd on the hills disclose
Gleams from a world in which the saints repose.

RYDAL

'By the Side of Rydal Mere' (an extract)

... Soft as a cloud is yon blue Ridge—the Mere
Seems firm as solid crystal, breathless, clear,
And motionless; and, to the gazer's eye,
Deeper than ocean, in the immensity
Of its vague mountains and unreal sky!
But, from the process in that still retreat,
Turn to minuter changes at our feet;
Observe how dewy Twilight has withdrawn
The crowd of daisies from the shaven lawn,
And has restored to view its tender green,
That, while the sun rode high, was lost beneath their
    dazzling sheen.
—An emblem this of what the sober Hour
Can do for minds disposed to feel its power!
Thus oft, when we in vain have wished away
The petty pleasures of the garish day,
Meek eve shuts up the whole usurping host
(Unbashful dwarfs each glittering at his post)
And leaves the disencumbered spirit free
To reassume a staid simplicity....

RYDAL

The garden of Rydal Mount, where the poet lived from 1813 to 1850, is a paradise of trees, flowering shrubs, flowers, sloping lawns and terraces, two of which were constructed entirely by the poet. The 'far terrace', as he called it, led to the boundary of the property, and beyond joined the public footpath to Grasmere. From the further end of this terrace, where he walked to and fro composing poetry, he had an unparalleled view of Rydal Water below.

The 'Far Terrace' of the Garden at Rydal Mount

The massy Ways, carried across these heights
By Roman perseverance, are destroyed
Or hidden under ground, like sleeping worms.
How venture then to hope that Time will spare
This humble Walk? Yet on the mountain's side
A Poet's hand first shaped it; and the steps
Of that same Bard—repeated to and fro
At morn, at noon, and under moonlight skies
Through the vicissitudes of many a year—
Forbade the weeds to creep o'er its grey line.
No longer, scattering to the heedless winds
The vocal raptures of fresh poesy,
Shall he frequent these precincts; locked no more
In earnest converse with beloved Friends,
Here will he gather stores of ready bliss,
As from the beds and borders of a garden
Choice flowers are gathered! But, if Power may spring
Out of a farewell yearning—favoured more
Than kindred wishes mated suitably
With vain regrets—the Exile would consign
This Walk, his beloved possession, to the care
Of those pure Minds that reverence the Muse.

– from *Inscriptions*

'Adieu, Rydalian Laurels! ...'

Adieu, Rydalian Laurels! that have grown
And spread as if ye knew that days might come
When ye would shelter in a happy home,
On this fair Mount, a Poet of your own,
One who ne'er ventured for a Delphic crown
To sue the God; but, haunting your green shade
All seasons through, is humbly pleased to braid
Ground-flowers, beneath your guardianship, self-sown.
Farewell! no Minstrels now with harp new-strung
For summer wandering quit their household bowers;

RYDAL

Yet not for this wants Poesy a tongue
To cheer the Itinerant on whom she pours
Her spirit, while he crosses lonely moors,
Or musing sits forsaken halls among.*

*Composed before going on a journey.

KIRKSTONE PASS

'The Pass of Kirkstone'
Within the mind strong fancies work,
A deep delight the bosom thrills
Oft as I pass along the fork
Of these fraternal hills:
Where, save the rugged road, we find
No appanage of human kind,
Nor hint of man; if stone or rock
Seem not his handy-work to mock
By something cognizably shaped;
Mockery—or model roughly hewn,
And left as if by earthquake strewn,
Or from the Flood escaped:
Altars for Druid service fit;
(But where no fire was ever lit,
Unless the glow-worm to the skies
Thence offer nightly sacrifice)
Wrinkled Egyptian monument;
Green moss-grown tower; or hoary tent;
Tents of a camp that never shall be razed—
On which four thousand years have gazed!

Ye ploughshares sparkling on the slopes!
Ye snow-white lambs that trip
Imprison'd mid the formal props
Of restless ownership!
Ye trees, that may tomorrow fall
To feed the insatiate Prodigal!
Lawns, houses, chattels, groves, and fields,
All that the fertile valley shields;
Wages of folly—baits of crime
Of life's uneasy game the stake,
Playthings that keep the eyes awake
Of drowsy, dotard Time;—
O care! O guilt!—O vales and plains,
Here, 'mid his own unvexed domains
A Genius dwells, that can subdue
At once all memory of You,—

KIRKSTONE PASS

Most potent when mists veil the sky,
Mists that distort and magnify,
While the coarse rushes to the sweeping breeze,
Sigh forth their ancient melodies!

List to those shriller notes!—*that* march
Perchance was on the blast,
When, through this Height's inverted arch
Rome's earliest legion passed!
—They saw, adventurously impelled,
And older eye than theirs beheld,
This block—and yon, whose church-like frame
Give to this savage Pass its name.
Aspiring Road! that lov'st to hide
Thy daring in a vapoury bourn,
Not seldom may the hour return
When thou shalt be my guide:
And I (as all men may find cause,
When life is at a weary pause,
And they have panted up the hill
Of duty with reluctant will)
Be thankful, even though tired and faint,
For the rich bounties of constraint;
Whence oft invigorating transports flow
That choice lacked courage to bestow!

My soul was grateful for delight
That wore a threatening brow;
A veil is lifted—can she slight
The scene that opens now?
Though habitation none appear,
The greenness tells, man must be there;
The shelter—that the perspective
Is of the clime in which we live;
Where Toil pursues his daily round;
Where Pity sheds sweet tears—and Love,
In woodbine bower or birchen grove,
Inflicts his tender wound.
—Who comes not hither ne'er shall know
How beautiful the world below;
Nor can he guess how lightly leaps
The brook adown the rocky steeps.
Farewell, thou desolate Domain!
Hope, pointing to the cultured plain,
Carols like a shepherd-boy;
And who is she?—Can that be Joy!
Who, with a sunbeam for her guide,
Smoothly skims the meadows wide;
While Faith, from yonder opening cloud,

KIRKSTONE PASS

To hill and vale proclaims aloud,
'Whate'er the weak may dread, the wicked dare,
Thy lot, O Man, is good, thy portion fair!'

BROTHERS WATER

· Northward from Kirkstone Pass the road descends to a bridge beside, on the left, Brothers Water. On one return journey to Rydal with his sister Dorothy in March 1802, Wordsworth stopped here, and sitting on the bridge, wrote these lines,

'The Cock is Crowing. . . .' (Written in March)

The cock is crowing,
The stream is flowing,
The small birds twitter,
The lake doth glitter,
The green field sleeps in the sun;
The oldest and youngest
Are at work with the strongest;
The cattle are grazing,
Their heads never raising;
There are forty feeding like one.

Like an army defeated
The snow hath retreated,
And now doth fare ill
On the top of the bare hill;
The Ploughboy is whooping—anon—anon:
There's joy in the mountains;
There's life in the fountains;
Small clouds are sailing,
Blue sky prevailing;
The rain is over and gone!

The simplicity of the poem is a sheer delight, conveying in a few lines excitement at the approach of Spring. Here is Dorothy's prose version of the occasion, lengthier and with attention for the minutiae of Nature, but conveying equally their *joie de vivre:* 'When we came to the foot of Brothers Water I left William sitting on the bridge and went along the path on the right side of the lake through the wood. I was delighted with what

BROTHERS WATER

I saw. The water under the boughs of the bare old trees, the simplicity of the mountains and the exquisite beauty of the path.... When I returned I found William writing a poem descriptive of the sights and sounds we saw and heard. There was a gentle flowing of the stream, the glittering lively lake, green fields without a living creature to be seen on them, behind us a flat pasture with 42 cattle feeding, to our left the road leading to the hamlet, no smoke there, the sun shone on the bare roofs. The people were at work ploughing, harrowing, and sowing—lasses spread dung, a dog's barking now and then, cocks crowing, birds twittering, the snow in the patches at the top of the highest hills, yellow palms, purple and green twigs on the birches, ashes with their glittering spikes quite bare, the hawthorn bright green with black stems under the oak. The moss of the oak glossy. We then went on passing two sisters at work, *they first passed us*, one with two pitch forks in her hand. The other had a spade. We had some talk with them. They laughed aloud after we were gone perhaps half in wantonness, half boldness.'

* * *

RIVER EDEN

'*The River Eden, Cumberland*'

Eden! till now thy beauty had I viewed
By glimpses only, and confess with shame
That verse of mine, whate'er its varying mood,
Repeats but once the sound of thy sweet name:
Yet fetched from Paradise that honour came,
Rightfully borne; for Nature gives thee flowers
That have no rivals among British bowers;
And thy bold rocks are worthy of their fame.
Measuring thy course, fair Stream! at length I pay
To my life's neighbour dues of neighbourhood;
But I have traced thee on thy winding way
With pleasure sometimes by this thought restrained—
For things far off we toil, while many a good
Not sought, because too near, is never gained.

LOWTHER

'Lowther'

Lowther! in thy majestic Pile are seen
Cathedral pomp and grace, in apt accord
With the baronial castle's sterner mien;
Union significant of God adored,
And charters won and guarded by the sword
Of ancient honour; whence that goodly state
Of polity which wise men venerate,
And will maintain, if God his help afford.
Hourly the democratic torrent swells;
For airy promises and hopes suborned
The strength of backward-looking thoughts is scorned.
Fall if ye must, ye Towers and Pinnacles,
With what ye symbolise; authentic Story
Will say, Ye disappeared with England's glory!

The Lowthers withheld payment of a debt owed to the Wordsworth family for many years, but when Sir James Lowther died, his son hastened to make amends. Ultimately, and ironically, William Lowther, Earl of Lonsdale, secured for Wordsworth the post of Distributor of Stamps for Westmorland. Lowther became his patron and friend, and the poet even went so far as to help the Tory lord with his political campaigns. The poet had once been a staunch Republican.

* * *

RIVER DUDDON

Unlike the rivers Eden and Lowther, the Duddon flows wild and free through high and rugged country, 1200 feet above sea level. Its source at Wrynose is above the pass leading to Hardknot, a route once used by the Romans. After flowing westward beside the road, the river turns south through Seathwaite, Dunnerdale, Ulpha to its mouth at Broughton-in-Furness. Wordsworth loved it for its unsullied, isolated beauty.

RIVER DUDDON

Child of the clouds! remote from every taint
Of sordid industry thy lot is cast;
Thine are the honours of the lofty waste:
Not seldom, when with heat the valleys faint
Thy handmaid Frost with spangled tissue quaint
Thy cradle decks;—to chant thy birth, thou hast
No meaner Poet than the whistling Blast,
And Desolation is thy Patron-saint!
She guards the ruthless Power! who would not spare
Those mighty forests, once the bison's screen,
Where stalked the hugh deer to his shaggy lair
Through paths and alleys roofed with darkest green;
Thousands of years before the silent air
Was pierced by whizzing shaft of hunter keen!

* * *

'Kirk of Ulpha'

The Kirk of Ulpha to the pilgrim's eye
Is welcome as a star, that doth present
Its shining forehead throught the peaceful rent
Of a black cloud diffused o'er half the sky:
Or as a fruitful palm-tree towering high
O'er the parched waste beside an Arab's tent;
Or the Indian tree whose branches, downward bent,
Take root again, a boundless canopy.
How sweet were leisure! could it yield no more
Than 'mid that wave-washed Churchyard to recline,
From pastoral graves extracting thoughts divine;
Or there to pace, and mark the summits hoar
Of distant moon-lit mountains faintly shine,
Soothed by the unseen River's gentle roar.

* * *

'Afterthought'

I thought of Thee, my partner and my guide,
As being past away.—Vain sympathies!
For, backward, Duddon! as I cast my eyes,
I see what was, and is, and will abide;
Still glides the Stream, and shall for ever glide;
The Form remains, the Function never dies;
While we, the brave, the mighty, and the wise,
We Men, who in our morn of youth defied
The elements, must vanish;—be it so!
Enough, if something from our hands have power
To live, and act, and serve the future hour;

RIVER DUDDON

And if, as toward the silent tomb we go,
Through love, through hope, and faith's transcendent dower,
We feel that we are greater than we know.
— sonnets from *The River Duddon* sequence.

EPILOGUE

From '*An Evening Walk*' (1793)

An Epistle in Verse to a Young Lady

Far from my dearest friend, 'tis mine to rove
Thro' bare grey dell, high wood, and pastoral cove;
His wizard course where hoary Derwent takes
Thro' craggs, and forest glooms, and opening lakes,
Staying his silent waves, to hear the roar
That stuns the tremulous cliffs of high Lodore:
Where the silver rocks the savage prospect chear
Of giant yews that frown on Rydale's mere;
Where peace to Grasmere's lonely island leads,
To willowy hedgerows, and to emerald meads;
Leads to her bridge, rude church, and cottag'd grounds,
Her rocky sheepwalks, and her woodland bounds;
Where, bosom'd deep, the shy Winander peeps
'Mid clust'ring isles, and holly-sprinkl'd steeps;
Where twilight glens endear my Esthwaite's shore,
And memory of departed pleasures, more.

Fair scenes! with other eyes, than once, I gaze,
The ever-varying charm your round displays,
Than when, erewhile, I taught, 'a happy child,'
The echoes of your rocks my carols wild:
Then did no ebb of cheerfulness demand
Sad tides of joy from Melancholy's hand;
In youth's wild eye the livelong day was bright,
The sun at morning, and the stars of night,
Alike, when first the vales the bittern fills,
Or the first woodcocks roam'd the moonlight hills.

Return Delights! with whom my road begun,
When Life was rear'd laughing up her morning sun;
When Transport kiss'd away my april tear,
'Rocking as in a dream the tedious year;'
When link'd with thoughtless Mirth I cours'd the plain,
And hope itself was all I knew of pain.

For then, ev'n then, the little heart would beat
At times, while young Content forsook her seat,
And wild Impatience, panting upward, show'd
Where tipp'd with gold the mountain-summits glow'd.
Alas! the idle tale of man is found
Depicted in the dial's moral round;
With Hope Reflexion blends her social rays
To gild the total tablet of his days;
Yet still, the sport of some malignant Pow'r,
He knows but from its shade the present hour.

While, Memory at my side, I wander here,
Starts at the simplest sight th'unbidden tear,
A form discover'd at the well-known seat,
A spot, that angles at the riv'lets feet,
The ray the cot of morning trav'ling nigh,
And sail that glides the well-known alders by.
But why, ungrateful, dwell on idle pain?
To shew her yet some joys to me remain,
Say, will my friend, with soft affection's ear,
The history of a poet's ev'ning hear?

When, in the south, the wan noon brooding still,
Breath'd a pale steam around the glaring hill,
And shades of deep embattl'd clouds were seen
Spotting the north cliffs with lights between;
Gazing the tempting shades to them deny'd,
When stood the shorten'd herds amid the tide,
Where, from the barren wall's unshelter'd end,
Long rails into the shallow lake extend;
When schoolboys stretch'd their length upon the green
And round the humming elm, a glittering scene!
In the brown park, in flocks, the troubl'd deer
Shook the still twinkling tail and glancing ear;
When horses in the wall-girt intake stood,
Unshaded, eying far below, the flood,
Crouded behind the swain, the mute distress,
With forward neck the closing gate to press;
And long, with wistful gaze, his walk survey'd,
Till dipp'd his pathway in the river shade;

—Then Quiet led me up the huddling rill,
Bright'ning with water-breaks the sombrous gill;
To where, while thick above the branches close,
In dark-brown bason its wild waves repose,
Inverted shrubs, and moss of darkest green,
Cling from the rocks, with pale wood-weeds between;
Save that, atop, the subtle sunbeams shine,
On wither'd briars that o'er the craggs recline;

Sole light admitted here, a small cascade,
Illumes with sparkling foam the twilight shade.
Beyond, along the visto of the brook,
Where antique roots its bustling path o'erlook;
The eye reposes on a secret bridge
Half grey, half shagg'd with ivy to its ridge.

—Sweet rill, farewel! Tomorrow's noon again,
Shall hide me wooing long thy wildwood strain;
But now the sun has gain'd his western road,
And eve's mild hour invites my steps abroad.

While, near the midway cliff, the silver'd kite
In many a whistling circle wheels her flight;
Slant wat'ry lights, from parting clouds a-pace,
Travel along the precipice's base;
Chearing it's naked waste of scatter'd stone
By lychens grey, and scanty moss o'er-grown,
Where scarce the foxglove peeps, and thistle's beard,
And desert stone-chat, all day long, is heard.

How pleasant, as the yellowing sun declines,
And with long rays and shades the landscape shines;
To mark the birches' stems all golden light,
That lit the dark slant wood with silvery white!
The willows weeping trees, that twinkling hoar,
Glanc'd oft upturn'd along the breezy shore,
Low bending o'er the colour'd water, fold
Their moveless boughs and leaves like threads of gold;
The skiffs with naked masts at anchor laid,
Before the boat-house peeping thro' the shade;
Th' unwearied glance of woodman's echo'd stroke;
And curling from the trees the cottage smoke.

Their pannier'd train a groupe of potters goad,
Winding from side to side up the steep road;
The peasant from yon cliff of fearful edge
Shot, down the headlong path way darts his sledge;
Bright beams the lonely mountain horse illume,
Feeding 'mid purple heath, 'green rings', and broom;
While the sharp slope the slacken'd team confounds,
Downward the pond'rous timber-wain resounds;
Beside their sheltering cross of wall, the flock
Feeds on in light, nor thinks of winter's shock;
In foamy breaks the rill, with merry song,
Dash'd down the rough rock, lightly leaps along;
From lonesome chapel at the mountain's feet,
Three humble bells their rustic chime repeat;

Sounds from the water-side the hammer'd boat;
And blasted quarry thunders heard remote.
Ev'n here, amid the sweep of endless woods.
Blue pomp of lakes, high cliffs, and falling floods,
Not undelightful are the simplest charms
Found by the verdant door of mountain farms.

Sweetly ferocious round his native walks,
Gaz'd by his sister-wives, the monarch stalks;
Spur-clad his nervous feet, and firm his tread,
A crest of purple tops his warrior head.
Bright sparks his black and haggard eyeball hurls
Afar, his tail he closes and unfurls;
Whose state, like pine-trees, waving to and fro,
Droops, and o'er canopies his regal brow,
On tiptoe rear'd he blows his clarion throat,
Threaten'd by faintly answering farms remote.

Bright'ning the cliffs between where sombrous pine,
And yew-trees o'er the silver rocks recline,
I love to mark the quarry's moving trains,
Dwarf-pannier'd steeds, and men, and numerous wains:
How busy the enormous hive within,
While Echo dallies with the various din!
Some hardly heard their chissel's clinking sound,
Toil, small as pigmies, in the gulph profound:
Some, dim between th' aërial cliffs descry'd,
O'erwalk the viewless plank from side to side;
These by the pale-blue rocks that ceaseless ring
Glad from their airy baskets hang and sing.

Hung o'er a cloud, above the steep that rears
It's edge all flame, the broad'ning sun appears;
A long blue bar its aegis orb divides.
And breaks the spreading of its golden tides;
And now it touches on the purple steep
That flings his shadow on the pictur'd deep,
Cross the calm lake's blue shades the cliffs aspire,
With tow'rs and woods a 'prospect all on fire;'
The coves and secret hollows thro' a ray
Of fainter gold a purple gleam betray;
The gilded turf arrays in richer green
Each speck of lawn the broken rocks between;
Deep yellow beams the scatter'd boles illume,
Far in the level forest's central gloom;
Waving his hat, the shepherd in the vale
Directs his winding dogs the cliffs to scale,
That, barking busy 'mid the glittering rocks,
Hunts, where he points, the intercepted flocks;